THIS BOOK BELONGS TO...

Name:	Age:

Favourite player:

2020/2021

My Predictions...	Actual...

The Canaries' final position:

The Canaries' top scorer:

Championship winners:

Championship top scorer:

FA Cup winners:

EFL Cup winners:

Contributor: Peter Rogers

A TWOCAN PUBLICATION

©2020. Published by twocan under licence from Norwich City FC.

Every effort has been made to ensure the accuracy of information within this publication but the publishers cannot be held responsible for any errors or omissions. Views expressed are those of the authors and do not necessarily represent those of the publishers or the football club. All rights reserved.

ISBN: 978-1-913362-32-4

PICTURE CREDITS:
Norwich City FC, Matthew Usher, Matthew Brasnett, Reuters, Rex Photography, Press Association.

£10

CONTENTS

1 TIM KRUL

POSITION: Goalkeeper   **DOB:** 03/04/1988
COUNTRY: Netherlands

Dutch international goalkeeper Tim Krul has displayed exceptional form for Norwich City following his arrival at Carrow Road on the eve of the 2018/19 season.

An ever-present Championship title-winner in his first season at the club, Krul's vast experience has been of particular benefit to the younger members of the City squad. The hero of Norwich's FA Cup fifth round penalty shoot-out victory at Tottenham Hotspur in March, Krul was voted the Canaries' Player of the Season for 2019/20.

MAX 2 AARONS

POSITION: Defender   **DOB:** 04/01/2000
COUNTRY: England

After enjoying a breakthrough season during the Canaries' 2018/19 Championship title-winning campaign, right-back Max Aarons was another of Norwich's young stars to shine at Premier League level in 2019/20.

A product of the Canaries' Academy, Aarons has swiftly developed a reputation as one of the very best right-backs in the country. He is already a regular with England at under-21 level.

3 SAM BYRAM

POSITION: Defender **DOB:** 16/09/1993
COUNTRY: England

Full-back Sam Byram joined the Canaries from West Ham United in the summer of 2019 ahead of the club's Premier League campaign.

With the ability to operate in either full-back berth, Byram's first Premier League start for the Canaries coincided with the memorable 3-2 victory over champions Manchester City at Carrow Road in September 2019. The former Leeds United and West Ham man made 20 appearances in all competitions for City last season.

GRANT 5 HANLEY

POSITION: Defender **DOB:** 20/11/1991
COUNTRY: Scotland

City skipper Grant Hanley saw injury limit him to just 15 Premier League outings in 2019/20.

Not having their leader available for large spells of the season was certainly a major blow for Daniel Farke's men. There is no doubting the Norwich defence always looks a more solid unit with Hanley at the heart of it. The experienced Scottish international brings priceless knowledge and know-how to the City backline.

CHRISTOPH ZIMMERMANN
6

POSITION: Defender **DOB:** 12/01/1993
COUNTRY: Germany

Giant German defender Christoph Zimmermann has become a popular character at Carrow Road since following head coach Daniel Farke from Borussia Dortmund ll to Norwich City in the summer of 2017.

A brave defender who is fully committed to the cause, Zimmermann has now made over a century of appearances for the Canaries and has often stepped up to captain the side in the absence of Grant Hanley.

7 LUKAS RUPP

POSITION: Midfielder   **DOB:** 08/01/1991
COUNTRY: Germany

Having represented a host of clubs in his homeland, German midfielder Lukas Rupp joined Norwich City in the January 2020 transfer window from Hoffenheim.

A neat technician who is always comfortable in possession, Rupp made his Canary debut in the 1-0 Premier League victory over Bournemouth at Carrow Road and went on to feature in 15 league and cup games for Norwich in 2019/20.

MARIO 8 VRANCIC

POSITION: Midfielder   **DOB:** 23/05/1989
COUNTRY: Bosnia & Herzegovina

A star performer in the closing months of Norwich's 2018/19 Championship title-winning campaign. Bosnia & Herzegovina international midfielder Mario Vrancic scored a number of memorable goals that etched his name into Carrow Road folklore.

Vrancic was limited to six starts at Premier League level last season and netted in the Canaries' entertaining 2-2 draw with Tottenham Hotspur at Carrow Road in December 2019.

JORDAN 9
HUGILL

POSITION: Striker   **DOB:** 04/06/1992
COUNTRY: England

Norwich City added to their attacking options for 2020/21 with the signing of striker Jordan Hugill from West Ham United in August 2020.

A proven Championship goalscorer with Preston North End, Hugill also netted an impressive 13 goals while on loan at Queens Park Rangers in 2019/20. The 6ft striker offers a physical presence to the Norwich frontline and will provide healthy competition for places at Carrow Road.

KIERAN 10
DOWELL

POSITION: Midfielder   **DOB:** 10/10/1997
COUNTRY: England

Attacking midfielder Kieran Dowell brings a wealth of Championship experience to the Canaries' squad following his July 2020 transfer from Everton to Carrow Road.

After progressing through the Toffees' Academy set-up, Dowell has gained valuable first team game-time with successful loan spells at Nottingham Forest, Sheffield United, Derby County and Wigan Athletic. An England under-21 international, Dowell marked his Norwich debut with a goal against Luton Town in the EFL Cup.

14 TODD CANTWELL

POSITION: Midfielder **DOB:** 27/03/1998
COUNTRY: England

Norfolk-born midfielder Todd Cantwell impressed during Norwich's Championship title-winning campaign in 2018/19 and then really grasped his opportunity to shine in the Premier League.

After progressing through the Academy age groups at Colney, Cantwell netted six Premier League goals last season and also struck a stunner in the Canaries' FA Cup quarter-final with Manchester United. He is another young Canary who has won international recognition with England under-21s.

PRZEMYSLAW 11 PLACHETA

POSITION: Midfielder **DOB:** 23/03/1998
COUNTRY: Poland

The arrival of Poland under-21 international Przemyslaw Placheta at Norwich City in July 2020 certainly sparked a great deal of excitement among the Norwich supporters.

Blessed with phenomenal pace, Placheta signed from Slask Wroclaw and agreed a four-year stay with the Canaries. His speed down the wing is sure to excite the fans and the summer recruit marked his home debut with the equalising goal in a 2-2 draw with Preston North End in September 2020.

XAVI 16
QUINTILLA

POSITION: Defender   **DOB:** 23/08/1996
COUNTRY: Spain

Along with fellow defender Ben Gibson, Spanish full-back Xavi Quintilla joined the Canaries in the summer of 2020 on a season-long loan with a view to a permanent transfer.

Signed from Villarreal, Quintilla offers both defensive stability and an appetitive to get forward and support attacks down the left flank. The former Spain youth international made his Canary debut in the opening day victory at Huddersfield Town.

EMILIANO **17**
BUENDIA

POSITION: Midfielder **DOB:** 25/12/1996
COUNTRY: Argentina

Born on Christmas Day 1996 - skilful Argentinean playmaker Emiliano Buendia has certainly been viewed as the perfect gift to Norwich fans following his arrival in 2018.

A highly-talented individual who possesses wonderful close control and quick thinking on the ball, Buendia was the creative spark in the Canaries' Championship title success two seasons ago. The little magician produced many great displays in the Premier League in 2019/20 and netted his first goal at that level against Watford.

18 MARCO
STIPERMANN

POSITION: Midfielder **DOB:** 09/02/1991
COUNTRY: Germany

Norwich City supporters will be hoping that Marco Stipermann can reproduce his Championship form of 2018/19 again this season as the Canaries bid to bounce back to the top flight.

As well as providing several assists for Teemu Pukki and others, Stipermann weighed in with nine league goals of his own in the title-winning campaign. With the ability to operate in a number of midfield roles and at full-back, Stipermann has a key role in the City squad.

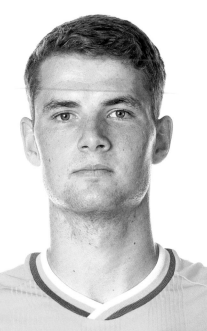

JACOB 19 SORENSEN

POSITION: Midfielder   **DOB:** 03/03/1998
COUNTRY: Denmark

A Denmark under-21 international, midfielder Jacob Sorensen joined the Canaries in the summer of 2020 and certainly appears to be a young player with a bright future in the game.

Having joined City on a three-year contract from Esbjerg fB, Sorensen has the physical attributes to win possession and the ability with the ball to dictate play and trigger forward moves.

19 OLIVER SKIPP

POSITION: Midfielder   **DOB:** 19/09/2000
COUNTRY: England

England under-21 international midfielder Oliver Skipp will spend the 2020/21 season on loan with the Canaries from Tottenham Hotspur.

City pulled off something of a coup to land Skipp's services with a host of other clubs also keen on the 20-year-old. With the strength and tackling ability to help protect the defence, Skipp also boasts an impressive range of passing skills and is certainly one to watch this season.

TEAM 2020/21

TEEMU 22 PUKKI

POSITION: Striker **DOB:** 29/03/1990
COUNTRY: Finland

Finnish international Teemu Pukki scored the goals that fired Norwich City to the Championship title in 2018/19 and Canary fans will be hoping he is right amongst the goals again this season.

The lethal marksman netted 29 Championship goals two seasons ago and was the Canaries' leading scorer again last season with eleven Premier League goals to his name. He opened his account for the new season with a rare headed effort in the 2-2 draw at home to Preston North End.

23 KENNY McLEAN

POSITION: Midfielder **DOB:** 08/01/1992
COUNTRY: Scotland

With 42 appearances in all competitions for the Canaries in 2019/20, no player featured in more games for City last season than Scotland international Kenny McLean.

Signed from Aberdeen, McLean began his career at St Mirren and joined the Canaries in January 2018. A hugely popular character with teammates and supporters, McLean's flexibility in the midfield roles are sure to see him remain one of the first names on Daniel Farke's teamsheet.

JOSHUA 24
MARTIN

POSITION: Midfielder   **DOB:** 09/09/2001
COUNTRY: England

An FA Youth Cup hat-trick against Newcastle United in January 2020 helped propel attacking midfielder Joshua Martin from the Canaries' Academy and into the thoughts of head coach Daniel Farke.

A bright attacking midfielder who loves to drift in from the left flank, Martin joined the Canaries having begun his youth career with Arsenal. After impressing while training with the first team squad, the teenager made his debut as a late substitute in City's Premier League match with Southampton in June 2020.

25 ONEL
HERNANDEZ

POSITION: Midfielder   **DOB:** 01/02/1993
COUNTRY: Cuba

The attacking instincts of flying winger Onel Hernandez have made the Cuba-born 27-year-old a crowd favourite at Carrow Road.

After playing a vital role in the Canaries' memorable Championship title triumph in 2018/19, Hernandez made history by becoming the first Cuban to play in the Premier League. His goal against Manchester United in October 2019 also saw him take the mantle of being the first Cuban to score at that level too.

TEAM 2020/21

BALI 26 MUMBA

POSITION: Defender   **DOB:** 08/10/2001
COUNTRY: DR Congo

A product of the Sunderland Academy, highly-rated teenager Bali Mumba left the Stadium of Light to join the Canaries in the summer of 2020.

With the ability to operate in central midfield or in a full-back berth, Mumba joined the Canaries for an undisclosed fee. A bright prospect with a great attitude, he progressed through the ranks at Sunderland to make nine first team appearances. His Canary debut came in the EFL Cup tie at Luton.

27 ALEXANDER TETTEY

POSITION: Midfielder   **DOB:** 04/04/1986
COUNTRY: Norway

Currently the longest-serving member of the City squad, Alex Tettey joined the Canaries back in 2012 from Rennes during Chris Hughton's reign as Norwich boss.

A tough-tackling defensive midfielder, Tettey has amassed almost 250 appearances for the club and has twice helped Norwich to win promotion to the Premier League. A scorer of some memorable goals, Tettey has gained cult status among the Carrow Road faithful.

MICHEAL 33 McGOVERN

POSITION: Goalkeeper **DOB:** 12/07/1984
COUNTRY: Northern Ireland

Experienced Northern Ireland international goalkeeper Michael McGovern provides valuable cover for Canaries' No1 Tim Krul.

A star performer for Northern Ireland, McGovern played a major role in his country's qualification for the finals of Euro 2016 and their success in reaching the knock-out stages. Having spent his entire club career in Scotland, Norwich became McGovern's first English club when he joined the Canaries in July 2016.

34 BEN GIBSON

POSITION: Defender **DOB:** 15/01/1993
COUNTRY: England

Central defender Ben Gibson joined the Canaries on a season-long loan from Premier League Burnley in September 2020.

Gibson gained a glowing reputation as a polished defender with Middlesbrough and was called into the England squad prior to his big money move to Turf Moor. The 27-year-old certainly brings a touch of class to the Norwich defence and the club have arrangements in place to sign him permanently should they gain promotion in 2020/21.

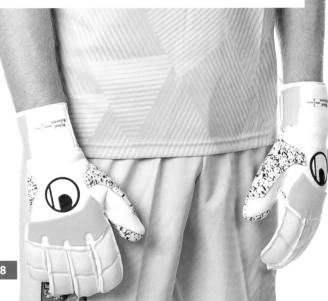

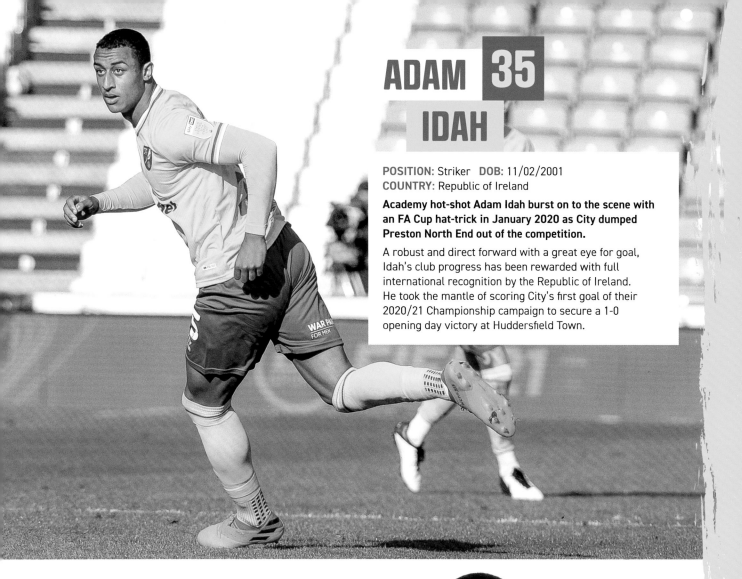

ADAM 35
IDAH

POSITION: Striker   **DOB:** 11/02/2001
COUNTRY: Republic of Ireland

Academy hot-shot Adam Idah burst on to the scene with an FA Cup hat-trick in January 2020 as City dumped Preston North End out of the competition.

A robust and direct forward with a great eye for goal, Idah's club progress has been rewarded with full international recognition by the Republic of Ireland. He took the mantle of scoring City's first goal of their 2020/21 Championship campaign to secure a 1-0 opening day victory at Huddersfield Town.

43 AKIN
FAMEWO

POSITION: Defender   **DOB:** 09/11/1998
COUNTRY: England

Defender Akin Famewo began his career with Luton Town and took in a loan spell with Grimsby Town before joining up with the Canaries' under-23 development squad in January 2019.

After making a positive impression at Colney, Famewo was named on the bench for City's Premier League match with Aston Villa in October 2019. He joined Scottish Premiership side St Mirren on loan in January 2020 before returning to Norwich and making his first team debut as a late substitute in the final game of the season at Manchester City.

PRZEMYSLAW
PLACHETA

SOCCER SKILLS

Great goalkeepers are an essential ingredient for successful teams in today's game. They have to excel in all areas of the art of keeping and Tim Krul is a great keeper that lives up to these expectations.

DISTRIBUTION
THE BASICS OF GOOD THROWING TECHNIQUE

OVERARM THROW

This is best for covering long distances. The body should be in line with the direction of the throw with the weight on the back foot. The ball should be brought forward in a bowling action with the arm straight.

JAVELIN THROW

This throw is made quickly with a low trajectory. The arm is bent for this throw, the ball is held beside the head and the body is in line with the direction of the throw. The arm is brought forward in a pushing movement with the ball being released at the top.

UNDERARM THROW

The ball is released from a crouching position, with a smooth underarm swing.

Throws do not usually travel as far as kicks but the greater speed and accuracy of throwing can make up for the lack of distance and will help the team retain possession. A player receiving a throw must be able to control it early.

Work hard at distribution and the benefits of this will be seen whenever you are in possession during a match.

EXERCISE ONE

Grab a friend and throw the ball to each other using the various throwing techniques at various distances apart.

EXERCISE TWO

The goalkeeper with the ball uses the various throws to knock another ball off a marker.

EXERCISE THREE

The goalkeepers try to throw the ball through the markers using various throwing techniques.

BOYS OF 1985

The 1984/85 season saw the Canaries make it a case of third time lucky at Wembley as Ken Brown's team tasted League Cup glory.

Having first won the trophy back in 1962, when the final was played over two legs, City had since reached the League Cup final in its Wembley format in both 1973 and 1975. On each occasion they suffered narrow 1-0 defeats to Tottenham Hotspur and Aston Villa respectively.

City's successful League Cup crusade began with a 9-4 aggregate victory over Preston

STAR PERFORMER

STEVE BRUCE

Forming an impressive partnership with Dave Watson at the heart of the Norwich defence, Steve Bruce enjoyed a memorable maiden campaign with the Canaries in 1984/85.

Shrewdly plucked from lower league Gillingham in the summer of 1984, Bruce was ever-present in the League Cup campaign and contributed three goals en route to the Wembley final.

His historic semi-final winner against Ipswich etched his name into Canary folklore and the central defender's performance in the Wembley final saw him voted Man of the Match. At the end of the season Bruce's contribution was further recognised when he collected the Barry Butler Memorial Trophy as City's Player of the Season.

North End. The Canaries then saw off the challenges of Aldershot Town and Notts County to tee-up a quarter-final tie away to Grimsby Town.

A single strike from John Deehan gave Norwich a 1-0 win on a bitterly cold night at Blundell Park which in turn set up the white-hot prospect of an East Anglian derby meeting with arch-rivals Ipswich Town in the semi-final.

Norwich suffered a 1-0 defeat in the first leg of the semi-final at Portman Road but turned on the style to record a never-to-be-forgotten 2-0 win in the return fixture at Carrow Road.

John Deehan levelled in the first half before Steve Bruce powered home a late bullet header from a Mark Barham corner at the Barclay End to send the Canaries to Wembley.

Sunderland provided the opposition in the final when a shot from City's Asa Hartford cannoned off defender Gordon Chisholm to separate the two sides and ultimately see the silverware head to Norfolk.

GOAL
OF THE SEASON

TEEMU PUKKI

V NEWCASTLE UNITED

AUGUST 2019

Ace marksman Teemu Pukki was the Canaries' leading goalscorer for a second consecutive season as the Finland international striker netted eleven Premier League goals in 2019/20.

As the club's top scorer, it will be of little surprise that Norwich City's Goal of the Season comes from the 'Pukki collection' with the Finn's stunning volley against Newcastle United, back in August 2019, taking the Canaries' prestigious award.

After hammering home 29 Championship goals to help fire Norwich City to the title in 2018/19, Pukki wasted little time in stepping up to the plate at Premier League level. He netted on his Premier League debut as City kicked off against Liverpool at Anfield. Pukki then followed up his Anfield strike with a never-to-be-forgotten Carrow Road hat-trick as City defeated Newcastle 3-1 on a sun-drenched August afternoon.

It was Pukki's 32nd-minute opener that proved to be the pick of the three as Carrow Road's first goal of the season ironically ended up being chosen as the best of the bunch for 2019/20.

After the visitors had failed to clear a corner, Pukki carefully watched a loose header drop before unleashing a thunderbolt volley high into the Newcastle net that left goalkeeper Martin Dubravka grasping at thin air. The strike was met with a roar of approval by an ecstatic home crowd who knew they had clearly witnessed a special goal.

With that delicious strike fresh in his mind, Pukki went on to add two second-half goals to complete his hat-trick. Firstly he doubled City's lead in the 63rd minute when he clinically finished off a neat passing move. He then rounded off the scoring after Todd Cantwell caught the visitors' defence cold, taking over to slot his third past a helpless Dubravka.

The Carrow Road faithful will certainly be hopeful of seeing plenty more memorable goals from their expert finisher in 2020/21.

Challenge your favourite grown-up and find out which of you is the biggest Championship brain!

ADULTS

Who is the only Championship club to have won the Premier League?

1 ANSWER

How many teams in the 2020/21 Championship have never competed in the Premier League?

2 ANSWER

Which former Leeds United and Norwich City midfielder currently plays for Middlesbrough?

3 ANSWER

At which Scottish club was QPR manager Mark Warburton once in charge?

4 ANSWER

Blackburn Rovers' manager Tony Mowbray previous played for and managed which Championship rival?

5

At which club did Sheffield Wednesday manager Garry Monk begin his managerial career?

6

From which club did Boro sign striker Britt Assombalonga?

7 ANSWER

Millwall manager Gary Rowett previously played for the Lions - true or false?

8 ANSWER

At which Championship ground will you find the Invincibles Stand?

9 ANSWER

In which year did Steve Cooper become Swansea City manager?

10 ANSWER

V KIDS

Which Championship club play their home games at Pride Park?

1 ANSWER

What is Sheffield Wednesday's nickname?

2

Which two clubs won automatic promotion to the Championship in 2019/20?

3 ANSWER

Ashton Gate is home to which Championship club?

4

Who is the manager of Cardiff City?

5

How many Welsh clubs are competing in the 2020/21 Championship?

6 ANSWER

Mark Warburton is the manager of which Championship team?

7 ANSWER

Which Championship stadium has the largest capacity?

8

How many Championship clubs have the word 'City' in their name?

9 ANSWER

What nationality is Preston manager Alex Neil?

10

27

Fill the page with your footy goals and dreams, no matter how big or small, and then start working on how to accomplish them!

We've started you off...

1. Visit Carrow Road

2. Complete 50 keepy-uppies

FOOTY BUCKET LIST

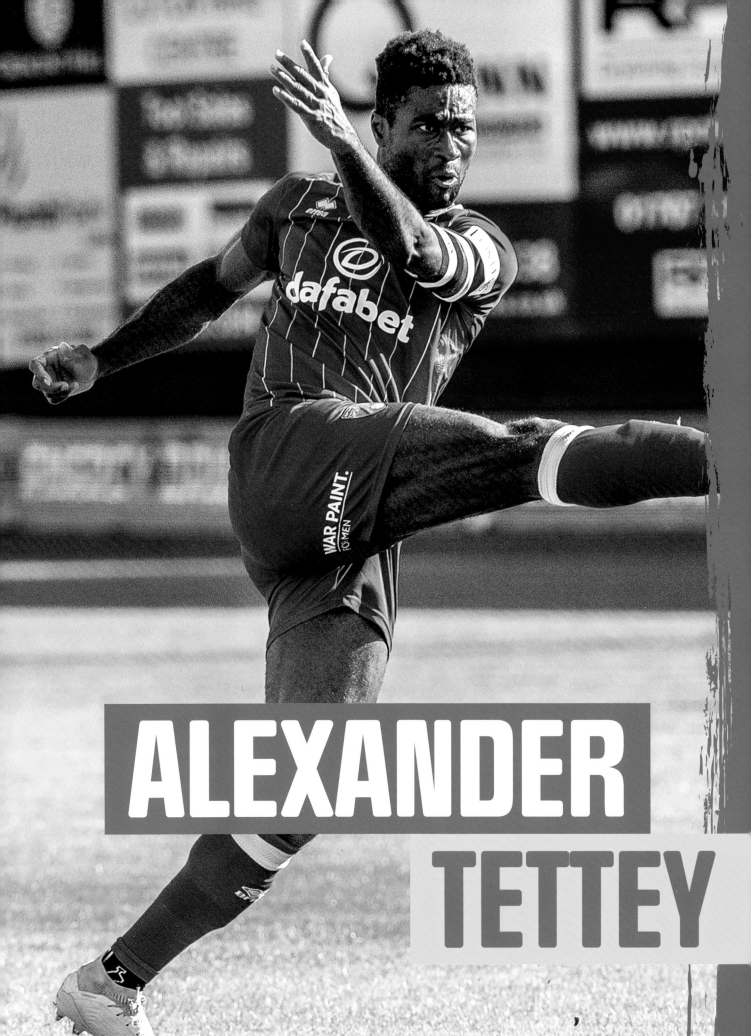

ALEXANDER
TETTEY

6

7

dafabet

WHO

Can you figure out the identity of all these Canaries stars?

8

IS IT?

9

10

ANSWERS ON PAGE 62

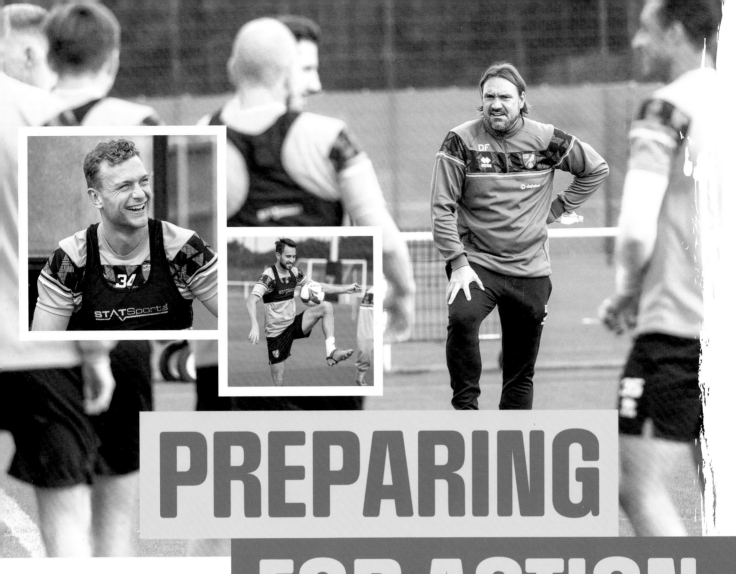

PREPARING FOR ACTION

Football matches may well be scheduled for 90 minutes but there are many days of preparation that go into making sure the players are at their physical and mental peak when they cross the white line to represent Norwich City.

Like all Championship clubs, the Canaries' pre-match planning is meticulous. The manager of course has final say as to who makes his starting line-up but the boss is ably assisted by a backroom staff of coaches, sports scientists, strength and conditioning experts, physiotherapists and nutritionists who all play their part in helping fine tune the players ahead of the manager's team selection.

The majority of the squads' preparations take place at the club's training ground and that all begins when the players report back for pre-season training.

Although the modern-day player has little down-time in terms of maintaining his overall fitness, pre-season really is a vital time for footballers to build themselves up to remain as fit, strong and healthy as possible for the challenging season that awaits.

The pre-season schedule often begins with a series of fitness tests. The results of those tests enables the club's coaching and fitness staff to assess each player's condition and level of fitness to ensure they are given the right work load during the pre-season programme.

When it comes to winning football matches, it is well known that both hard work and practice are two essential ingredients to success. However, in terms of strength and fitness, then rest, recovery and diet also have crucial parts to play in a footballer's wellbeing.

The modern game now sees technology playing its part in training too - prior to beginning their training sessions, the players are provided with a GPS tracking system and heart rate analysis monitors ensuring that all that they do in a training session can be measured, monitored and reviewed.

On-pitch training drills and gym work is now enhanced further with players often taking part in yoga and pilates classes while always receiving expert advice in terms of their diet, rest and mental welfare.

TIM
KRUL

SOCCER SKILLS

DEFENDING

Defending is an art - not as spectacular as swerving a free kick around the wall into the net or floating a crossfield pass into the path of an oncoming wingback - but nevertheless, just as important. Every successful team has a solid defence and can defend as a team.

Defenders must also master the art of defending one on one...

EXERCISE ONE

Two adjacent 10m x 10m grids have two players, X and Y at the opposite ends of the grids. X plays the ball to Y, who is then allowed to attack defender X with the ball. Y's target is to be able to stop the ball, under control, on the opposite end line. Defender X has to try to stop this happening. Y is encouraged to be direct and run at X with the ball.

KEY FACTORS

1. Do not approach the attacker square on. Adopt a sideways stance which enables rapid forward and backwards movement.

2. Do not dive in. Be patient and wait for your opponent to make a mistake. Always be on your toes.

3. Threaten the ball without actually committing to a tackle. Pretending to tackle can often panic the opponent!

4. Tackle when you are sure you will win it!

EXERCISE TWO

Here the game is progressed to a two v two situation when X1 and X2 play as a team against Y1 and Y2.

The same target is used for this game - the players have to stand on the opposite line with the ball, either by dribbling past their opponents or by passing the ball through them.

The same key factors are relevant here with the addition of two more:

5. Covering your defending partner when he is being attacked.

6. Communication between the two defenders is vital.

If a team can get these points of defending right, throughout the side, they will become very difficult to beat.

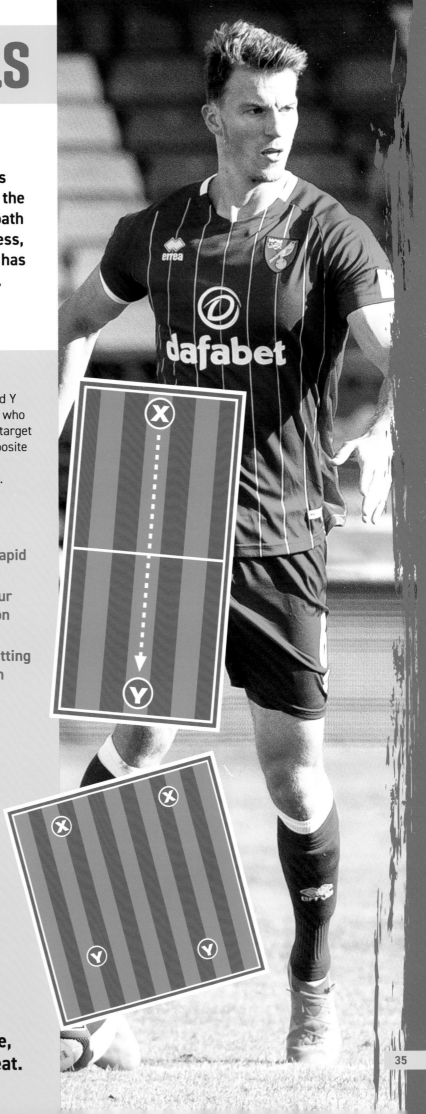

Take our quick-fire personality test to see where Daniel Farke would utilise your skills in the Canaries' line-up...

WHICH FOOTBALLER ARE YOU?

1. What is your favourite activity at the park?

a. Leaping around
b. Practicing my heading
c. Lots of non-stop running
d. Scoring goals

2. What is your biggest strength?

a. My height
b. My strength
c. My stamina
d. My speed

3. Which would you rather win?

a. A game of catch
b. A weight lifting contest
c. A long distance run
d. A sprint race

4. You score a goal! How do you celebrate?

a. I turn and punch the air
b. I clench my fist in delight
c. I high-five a teammate
d. I slide on my knees

5. How would the opposition describe you?

a. Hard to beat
b. Determined to succeed
c. All-action
d. Lethal in front of goal

6. What's your favourite move?

a. Springing high to catch under pressure
b. A sliding tackle
c. Playing the perfect through ball
d. Spinning away from my marker

7. What is the key to winning a game?

a. Keeping a clean sheet

b. Winning your individual battles

c. Maintaining possession

d. Taking chances that come your way

8. What is your favourite number?

a. One

b. Five

c. Seven

d. Nine

9. How would you describe your style of play?

a. Disciplined

b. Fully committed

c. Relentless

d. Technically gifted

10. What do your teammates call you?

a. Secure

b. Reliable

c. Energetic

d. Mr/Miss goals

MOSTLY As

You would clearly be a safe pair of hands in goal. Watch out Tim Krul, there's competition here for the No1 shirt!

MOSTLY Bs

Sounds like you are a young Max Aarons in the making - there could well be a role for you in the City back four...

MOSTLY Cs

You could comfortably take your place in the heart of midfield and help make things tick at Carrow Road. Move over Kieran Dowell!

MOSTLY Ds

Looks like we have a budding Jordan Hugill on our hands! Who do you fancy partnering in attack?

BOYS OF 1993

Norwich City's team of 1992/93 proved to be the season's real surprise package as Mike Walker's men took the inaugural Premier League campaign by storm.

Walker had been promoted from reserve team boss to first team manager in the summer. The appointment of a rookie manager and the departure of star striker and crowd favourite Robert Fleck to Chelsea in a big money move all resulted in the Canaries being among the favourites for relegation.

When Walker's men found themselves 2-0 down at half-time on the opening day of the season,

STAR PERFORMER

MARK ROBINS

Ace goal-getter Mark Robins was signed from Manchester United for a fee of £800,000 on the eve of the 1993/94 season following the sale of Robert Fleck to Chelsea.

Robins wasted little time in making his mark for the Canaries. His two-goal debut at Arsenal on opening day inspired a 4-2 victory and the striker then marked his home debut with a expertly executed goal to seal a 2-1 win over Chelsea.

In total, Robins netted 15 Premier League goals in his first season at Carrow Road including a memorable hat-trick on his return to the north west as City won 3-2 away to Oldham Athletic.

the weeks and months ahead looked like being an uphill challenge for the Canaries. However, the second-half introduction of new signing Mark Robins from Manchester United suddenly changed the outlook. Robins soon reduced the arrears at Highbury before goals from David Phillips, Ruel Fox and a second from Robins completed the most unexpected of turnarounds.

Full of confidence from their 4-2 win at Arsenal, City flew to the top of the Premier League table with a string of impressive results and performances. As the season progressed Norwich remained in a three-way battle for the title with Manchester United and Aston Villa.

The season ended with United taking the title and City securing their highest-ever league finish of third in the top flight. That third place spot proved enough to bring European football to Carrow Road for the first time the following season and saw Norwich face Vitesse Arnhem, Bayern Munich and Inter Milan in the UEFA Cup.

COLOURING IN

CHALLENGE

ADAM
IDAH

PLAYER OF THE SEASON

TIM KRUL

Goalkeeper Tim Krul capped off an impressive second season with the Canaries by landing the Barry Butler Memorial Trophy as Norwich City's Player of the Season for 2019/20.

The Dutch international keeper also saw his impressive club form earn him a return to the Netherlands national squad despite the Canaries relegation from the Premier League.

After seeing Krul pull off numerous spectacular saves, the Norwich fans voted him their top performing Canary ahead of Todd Cantwell and Alex Tettey in an end-of-season poll.

City's number one made 38 appearances in all competitions in 2019/20, with highlights from an individual standpoint including two penalty saves against Manchester United at Carrow Road and a heroic display in the FA Cup fifth round penalty shoot-out triumph over Tottenham Hotspur in March.

Krul became the fifth City goalkeeper to receive the Barry Butler Memorial Trophy after Kevin Keelan, Chris Woods, Bryan Gunn and Andy Marshall.

After learning of his award, Krul acknowledged what a great honour it was to see his name added to the list of Norwich City greats on the plinth of the famous club trophy.

"It's a big honour. To be part of the history of the club is special," said Krul.

"I know Bryan Gunn very well, he's a legend here. I had the honour to meet Kevin Keelan in Tampa Bay as well," he added. "In years to come, I'll look back on this trophy and realise in a few years how special it is."

YOUNG PLAYER OF THE SEASON

TODD CANTWELL

Pipped by goalkeeper Tim Krul to the Barry Butler Memorial Trophy, midfielder Todd Cantwell was certainly Norwich City's Young Player of the Season for 2019/20.

The 22-year-old Norfolk-born midfielder made 24 Championship appearances in the Canaries' 2018/19 title-winning campaign before taking the Premier League by storm last season.

An exciting attack-minded player, Cantwell was able to create goalscoring opportunities for others in 2019/20 plus net six top-flight goals of his own, including memorable strikes against Chelsea, Manchester City and Everton.

There are five Captain Canaries hiding in the crowd as Norwich fans celebrate scoring against Birmingham City in their 2-0 victory in 1998. Can you find him?

CLASSIC
FANTASTIC

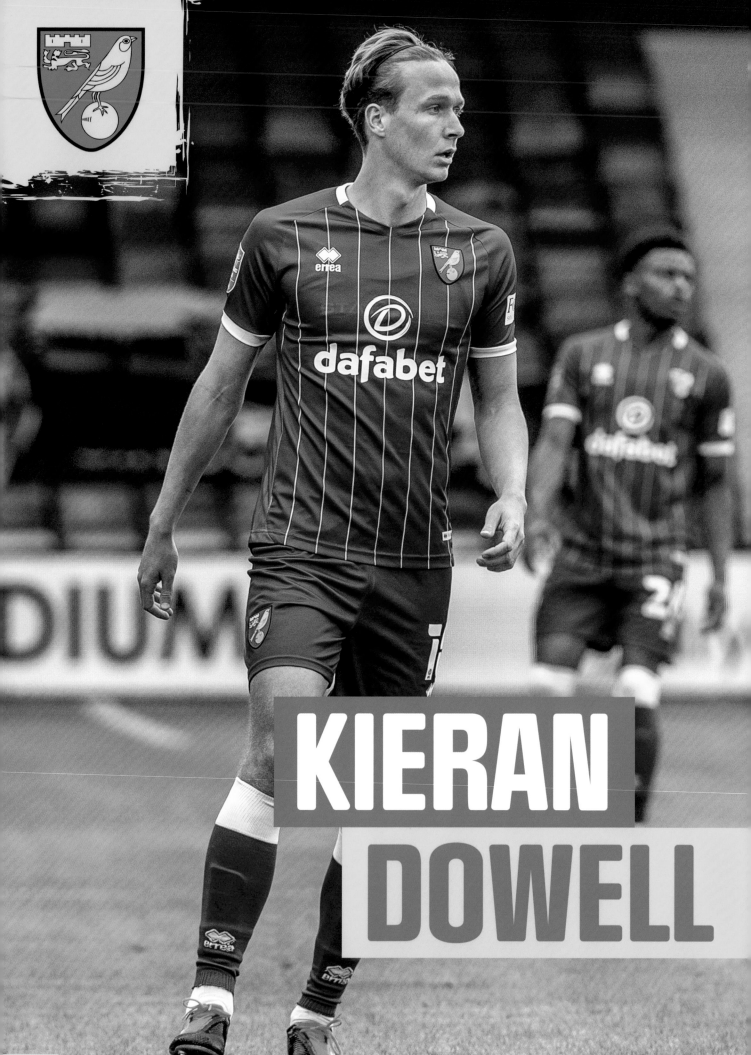

KIERAN
DOWELL

Can you find the eight differences between these two photos?

SPOT THE DIFFERENCE

What are your predictions for the 2020/21 season?

2020/21

PREMIER LEAGUE

YOUR PREDICTION FOR PREMIER LEAGUE WINNERS:

YOUR PREDICTION FOR PREMIER LEAGUE RUNNERS-UP:

CHAMPIONSHIP

YOUR PREDICTION FOR CHAMPIONSHIP WINNERS:

YOUR PREDICTION FOR CHAMPIONSHIP RUNNERS-UP:

TOP SCORERS

**YOUR PREDICTION
FOR PREMIER LEAGUE TOP SCORER:**

**YOUR PREDICTION
FOR CHAMPIONSHIP TOP SCORER:**

FA CUP & EFL CUP

**YOUR PREDICTION
FOR FA CUP WINNERS:**

**YOUR PREDICTION
FOR EFL CUP WINNERS:**

PREDICTIONS

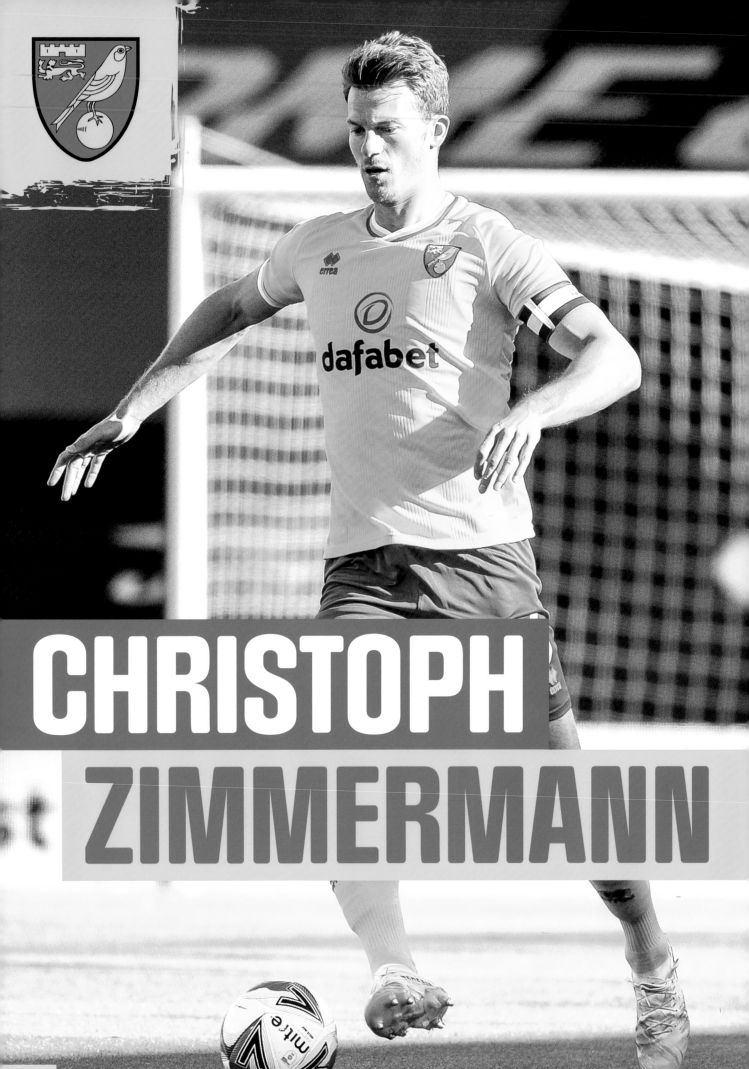

CHRISTOPH
ZIMMERMANN

SOCCER SKILLS
CHEST CONTROL

Controlling the ball quickly and with minimum fuss in order to get the ball where you want it, so you can pass or shoot, can be the difference between a good player and a top class player.

EXERCISE ONE

Grab two of your mates to start the exercise. A and C stand 10yds apart and have a ball each, ready to act as servers.

B works first. B must run towards A who serves the ball for B to control with the chest and pass back to A. B then turns, runs to C and repeats the exercise.

Once B has worked for 30 seconds all the players rotate.

KEY FACTORS

1. Look to control the ball as early as possible.
2. Get in line with the ball.
3. Keep eyes on the ball.
4. Relax the body on impact with the ball to cushion it.

EXERCISE TWO

In this exercise there are 5 servers positioned around a 15yd square. At one side of the square there is a goal.

T starts in the middle of the square. S1 serves first, throwing the ball in the air towards T. T must control the ball with the chest and try to shoot past the goalkeeper, as soon as T has shot on goal they must prepare for the next serve from S2.

Once T has received a ball from every server the players rotate positions - the same key factors apply.

Players who can control a ball quickly, putting the ball in a position for a shot or pass, give themselves and their teammates the extra valuable seconds required in today's intense style of play.

Challenge your favourite grown-up and find out which of you is the biggest Championship brain!

ADULTS

Prior to moving to the Madejski Stadium, where did Reading play their home matches?

11 ANSWER

Which kit manufacturer produces Queens Park Rangers' 2020/21 playing strip?

12 ANSWER

At which Championship club did Preston goalkeeper Declan Rudd begin his career?

13 ANSWER

What nationality is Millwall goalkeeper Bartosz Bialkowski?

14 ANSWER

At which club did Coventry City manager Mark Robins begin his managerial career?

15 ANSWER

Who did Garry Monk succeed as Sheffield Wednesday boss in 2019?

16 ANSWER

What was the name of Derby County's former ground?

17 ANSWER

Cardiff City midfielder Will Vaulks plays international football for which country?

18 ANSWER

Who is the captain of Stoke City?

19 ANSWER

From which club did Preston North End sign Scott Sinclair?

20 ANSWER

V KIDS

PART 2

The adults' questions are on the left page and the kids' questions are on the right page.

Who is the manager of Reading?

11 ANSWER

Wayne Rooney plays for which Championship club?

12

With which country is Norwich goalkeeper Tim Krul a full international?

13 ANSWER

Which club's nickname is 'The Lions'?

14

Which country did Stoke City manager Michael O'Neill guide to finals of Euro 2016?

15

What nationality is Norwich City manager Daniel Farke?

16

Rammie and Ewie are the official mascots of which Championship club?

17

Queens Park Rangers are famous for playing in what type of shirts?

18

Which Championship team play their home matches at Ewood Park?

19 ANSWER

Who is the manager of Rotherham United?

20

BOYS OF 2010

Having suffered a slump to the club's lowest ebb in 50 years, Norwich City's class of 2009/10 made a swift return to English football's second tier as they romped to the League One title.

The 2009/10 campaign saw the club playing league fixtures outside of the top two divisions for the first time since 1959/60 and after suffering a horrendous 7-1 home defeat to Colchester United on opening day the road back to the Championship certainly looked a long one.

However a swift change of manager saw Paul Lambert, the man who oversaw Colchester's shock triumph at Carrow Road, head to Norfolk and change the Canaries' fortunes.

STAR PERFORMER
GRANT HOLT

A summer signing by then Norwich boss Bryan Gunn, striker Grant Holt was charged with firing the goals to take Norwich City back to the Championship.

Installed as captain by new boss Paul Lambert early in the 2009/10 season, Holt swiftly set about repaying his transfer fee with goals galore. A powerful striker with a great eye for goal - the former Shrewsbury Town man netted a total of 30 goals in his debut season at Carrow Road (24 in the league) as Norwich cruised to the title.

An extremely popular player with supporters and teammates, Holt ended the 2009/10 campaign as Player of the Season. His goals proved vital to the success that followed for the club over the coming seasons.

With Lambert installed in the home dugout the Canaries never looked back. The Scot re-motivated the squad and introduced a real desire for success.

He also created a three-pronged attack of Grant Holt, Chris Martin and Wes Hoolahan which proved far too hot for League One to handle.

Despite their troubled start to the campaign, by the turn of the year Norwich were in the automatic promotion places and nothing was going to stop them.

Revenge over Colchester for that opening-day defeat was gained with a 5-0 win in the return fixture. Promotion rivals Leeds United were then defeated 1-0 at Carrow Road thanks to a brilliant diving header from Chris Martin before promotion was secured away to Charlton Athletic. After defeating Gillingham at Carrow Road, Norwich were League One champions with two games to spare.

The arrival of Lambert as Norwich manager was the catalyst for the League One title triumph and signalled the beginning of a truly remarkable three-year period in Norwich City history.

JARGON BUSTER

Here is a list of footy jargon. All but one of the terms are hidden in the grid...

...can you work out which is missing?

All To Play For

Back Of The Net

Bags Of Pace

Big Game Player

Box-To-Box

Class Act

Debut

Derby Day

Early Doors

Funny Old Game

Game Of Two Halves

Hat-Trick

Header

Hollywood Pass

Keep It Tight

Massive Game

Midfield General

Natural Goalscorer

Row Z

Worldy

```
A S M Z U C E M A G E V I S S A M
V A W T B X O W A C V T S V Y B N
P O I B Y H E A D E R A V B R Q A
R L Q C J K X Z E F M L F J N E T
O G F W K C I R T T A H C S A Z U
E X B H D A V A P N H X G B J E R
T K A L L T O P L A Y F O R D C A
I R C P M E Q M O L R X G H O A L
F L K D N U R A S T T P K Q C P G
U F O N Z Y D I W O M W Y I B F O
N H F W Z O E S B B U N E H L O A
N J T G O B N O D F F X K A D S L
Y Z H S V R X M A G V O R N I G S
O X E A D C L H H G A E U G Z A C
L B N K Q J L D C J N K A C I B O
D D E R B Y D A Y E E S P B L B R
G W T E U O I P G J I O J G S M E
A C I O K I R D Y U X K T S F A R
M H W V Y B L T B P C H F O R R A
E O P C D E E T G E G Q B L P E N
V G C M I H A F M I E K Y V Z G L
H J B F D W A R T X I D H D C T D
L X D M O A S T A S O L G A T C R
V I A Q K Y I H S O D W J H Y A Q
M P F E Z P R G R G U N F M I S G
Z I N Q E J N S L J P I K Z Y S O
D B S E V L A H O W T F O E M A G
E K T X S L T E M X K W U L L I
U S N Q L U W E A B V R S P C O
A Y O D E B U T W Y O T A N B M
H O L L Y W O O D P A S S U T I
```

ANSWERS ON PAGE 62

ONEL HERNANDEZ

Want to leap like Tim Krul, have the strength of Max Aarons or boast the endurance of Lukas Rupp? Build up your strength for action with our...

30 DAY

Day 1
Right let's get started! 10 squats, 25 star jumps, 10 sit-ups - all before school!

Day 2
Make your mum a brew before going out to practice your keepy-uppys

Day 3
10 squats
50 star jumps
10 sit-ups

Day 4
How about swapping the crisps in your lunchbox for an apple?

Day 5
Take a one mile ride on your bike

Day 6
75 star jumps
15 sit-ups
15 press-ups

Day 7
Help clean the car before going out to play headers and volleys with your friends

Day 8
75 star jumps
15 sit-ups
15 press-ups
Before and after school now!

Day 9
Walk to school rather than take the bus

Day 10
Head to the swimming pool for a 30-minute swim

Day 11
100 star jumps
20 sit-ups
20 press-ups
Twice a day now, don't forget!

Day 12
Make sure you trade one of your fizzy drinks for a glass of water today

Day 13
Jog to the shop for your mum... before playing any video games!

Day 14
Give a hand around the house before kicking your ball against the wall 500 times

Day 15
Time to increase those exercises!
25 squats
25 sit-ups
25 press-ups
Before and after school!

Day 16
Take a nice paced two-mile jog today

Day 17
25 squats
150 star jumps
25 press-ups
Remember, before and after school

Day 18
Cycle to school rather than rely on the bus or a lift

Day 19
30 squats
150 star jumps
30 press-ups
Twice a day too!

Day 20
Get out and practice those free-kicks, practice makes perfect remember...

Day 21
Get peddling! Time for a two-mile trip on two wheels today

Day 22
Upping the workload now...
40 squats, 40 sit-ups
40 press-ups
Before and after school!

Day 23
Wave goodbye to the chips - ask for a nice salad for lunch today

Day 24
40 squats
40 sit-ups
40 press-ups
Twice a day, don't forget...

Day 25
Time to get pounding the streets - the jogging is up to three miles today

Day 26
45 star jumps
45 sit-ups
45 press-ups

Day 27
Time to swap those sweets and biscuits for some fruit

Day 28
45 star jumps
45 sit-ups
45 press-ups

Day 29
You're getting fitter and fitter now! Keep up the squats and star jumps plus join an after-school sports club - ideally football!

Day 30
Well done - you made it!
50 squats, 50 sit-ups and 50 press-ups!
These are the core ingredients to your success

CHALLENGE
to improve your all-round footy fitness!

Can you figure out what ball is the real one in each photo?

WHAT BALL?

LUKAS
RUPP

ANSWERS

PAGE 26 · ADULTS V KIDS

Adults

1. Blackburn Rovers. 2. Seven - Brentford, Bristol City, Luton Town, Millwall, Preston North End, Rotherham United and Wycombe Wanderers. 3. Jonny Howson. 4. Glasgow Rangers. 5. Middlesbrough. 6. Swansea City. 7. Nottingham Forest. 8. False. 9. Deepdale, Preston North End. 10. 2019.

Kids

1. Derby County. 2. The Owls. 3. Coventry City and Rotherham United. 4. Bristol City. 5. Neil Harris. 6. Two, Cardiff City and Swansea City. 7. QPR. 8. Hillsborough, Sheffield Wednesday. 9. Seven - Birmingham City, Bristol City, Cardiff City, Coventry City, Norwich City, Stoke City and Swansea City. 10. Scottish.

PAGE 30 · WHO IS IT?

1. Kenny McLean. 2. Christoph Zimmermann.
3. Kieran Dowell. 4. Joshua Martin.
5. Jordan Hugill. 6. Xavi Quintilla.
7. Teemu Pukki. 8. Todd Cantwell.
9. Bali Mumba. 10. Marco Stiepermann.

PAGE 44
CLASSIC FANTASTIC ⟶

PAGE 47
SPOT THE DIFFERENCE ⟶

PAGE 52 · ADULTS V KIDS

Adults

11. Elm Park. 12. Errea. 13. Norwich City.
14. Polish. 15. Rotherham United. 16. Steve Bruce. 17. The Baseball Ground. 18. Wales.
19. Ryan Shawcross. 20. Celtic.

Kids

11. Veljko Paunović. 12. Derby County. 13. Holland.
14. Millwall. 15. Northern Ireland. 16. German.
17. Derby County. 18. Blue and white hoops.
19. Blackburn Rovers. 20. Paul Warne.

PAGE 56 · JARGON BUSTER

Big Game Player.

PAGE 60 · WHAT BALL?

TOP: Ball D.
BOTTOM: Ball F.